1941-1945

Przemyslaw Budzbon

Dedication: To Eva

Front cover illustration:
The destroyer *Razyaryonnyi*; see
plate 23

Back cover illustrations:
Top: *G5*-class motor torpedo-
boats; see plate 61.
Bottom: The battleship *Marat*;
see plate 1.

1. In the 1920s the Russian
Navy had three battleships,
survivors of the *Gangut* Class.
During the 1930s they
underwent 'face-lifting'
modernization which although
extending the battlefleet's life
did little to enhance their
inadequate protection. *Marat*
(namesake of the modernized
class, she being the first to be
taken in hand) is seen here
during the 1937 Coronation
Review at Spithead, showing her
outdated layout which
originated from Admiral
Cunniberti's design of 1908.
(Imperial War Museum, Neg No.
MH7)

SOVIET NAVY AT WAR 1941-1945

Przemyslaw Budzbon

ARMS AND
ARMOUR

2. In June 1941 the Russian Navy had approximately 290,000 personnel on active service; this number had increased to 415,000 by June 1943 and to 600,000 by May 1945. The photograph shows Russian sailors fighting ashore; besides the Naval Infantry, which totalled some 100,000 men, almost 390,000 sailors (not included in the above list) were deployed ashore; they suffered heavy losses because of a lack of field training.

3. On 23 September 1941 German dive-bombers damaged *Marat* at Kronshtadt. A bomb ignited the torpedo magazine and in the resulting explosion the forward part of the hull as far as the forefunnel was destroyed and sank. The remainder of the ship was intact and, following provisional repairs during the winter of 1941-2, she was employed as a floating battery (shown here); from May 1943 she sailed under her original name *Petropavlovsk*.

▲2 ▼3

INTRODUCTION

First published in Great Britain in 1989 by Arms and Armour Press, Artillery House, Artillery Row, London SW1P 1RT.

Distributed in the USA by Sterling Publishing Co. Inc., 2 Park Avenue, New York, NY 10016.

Distributed in Australia by Capricorn Link (Australia) Pty. Ltd., P.O. Box 665, Lane Cove, New South Wales 2066, Australia.

British Library Cataloguing in Publication Data:
Budzbon, Przemyslaw
Soviet Navy at war 1941–1945
1. Naval operations by Union of Soviet Socialist Republics Voenno-Morskoi
Flott. Strategy. History
I. Title.   II. Series
359.4'.3'.0947
ISBN 0-85368-948-2

Line drawings by the author.

Designed and edited by DAG Publications Ltd. Designed by David Gibbons; edited by Michael Boxall; layout by Anthony A. Evans; typeset by Ronset Typesetters Ltd, Darwen, Lancashire, and by Typesetters (Birmingham) Limited, Warley, West Midlands; camerawork by M&E Reproductions, North Fambridge, Essex; printed and bound in Great Britain by The Alden Press Limited, Oxford.

On the morning of 22 June 1941 the Soviet Union was invaded by German forces, thereby shattering Stalin's long-term ambition – the conquest of Europe after the belligerent powers had bled themselves white, and become easy victims. The Russian armed forces were caught unprepared for major warfare; a large rearmament programme was under way, and the high command had been decimated in the great purges of 1937-8.

The Navy comprised 470 warships and 670 minor vessels divided between the Baltic, Black Sea, Barents Sea and Pacific Fleets, with flotillas in the Caspian Sea and on the Rivers Amur, Danube and Prypyat. A further 219 major warships in various stages of construction were evidence of an ambitious desire to create an ocean-going navy under the third Five-Year Plan of 1938-43.

Since the struggle against the Germans was decided by land campaigns, the Navy's influence was only marginal – activity being concentrated on support of the armies and attempts to cut the sea lanes in the vicinity of land fronts. Following heavy losses during the withdrawals from the Baltic and the Black Seas, the Russians were unwilling to risk larger surviving units whose maintenance in besieged Leningrad or small Caucasian ports was therefore often neglected.

The entire burden of the surface naval war was now borne by the 'mosquito' fleet: minesweepers, motor boats, patrol craft and 1,300 mercantile conversions – adapted trawlers, tugs and riverine vessels. These were used in all environments – open sea, lakes and rivers – and for all sorts of duties throughout the war, and they suffered heavy losses.

Operating with varying intensity and success, these light forces made little impact on the German convoy system. The Russian submarine arm, dogged by technical shortcomings and often inadequately trained crews, was unable to impede even training manoeuvres conducted by U-boats in the central Baltic. In fact, it was only the strength of the land offensive in 1944-45 that enabled the Baltic Fleet to deploy in this area at all.

During the two weeks of war against Japan, in September 1945, the Pacific Fleet (strengthened by US-supplied ships) successfully executed assaults against ports in Korea and southern Sakhalin, and in the Kurile Islands. No opposition was encountered, the Japanese Navy having been annihilated by the Allies.

On VJ-Day the Russian Navy comprised 530 warships and 1,700 minor vessels of which some 88 and 1,000 respectively had been built in home yards during the war, while 166 and 340 respectively had been supplied under Lend-Lease. Although most of the Russian ships were obsolescent or worn out, equipment obtained from the Allies during the war, and the ships captured from the Germans in 1945 together provided a solid base from which was developed a modern, sophisticated navy within the next four decades.

The photographs in this book have been assembled from collections owned by the Imperial War Museum, London (negative numbers of IWM pictures are given and prints can be ordered from the museum); National Archives and Records, Washington, DC; Aldo Fraccaroli in Switzerland; Boris V. Lemachko in the Soviet Union; Jerzy Micinski and Marek Twardowski in Poland; Adrian Vicary in Norfolk, England; and the Author.

▲4

4. *Sevastopol* seen just after the war, carrying British radars and increased AA armament. As a sop to Stalin's ocean-going naval ambitions, the Russian battleships remained in front-line service well into the 1950s. Their evident obsolescence was turned to good account in official publications which praised the genius of Russian shipwrights who could turn out ships with a lifespan of more than forty years, while ships built in capitalist countries had long since gone to the breakers. Not until after Stalin's death were they relegated to training duties and in February 1956 they were ordered to the breakers by Admiral Gorshkov during only his sixth week as Commander-in-Chief of the Navy.

5. The decision to build an ocean-going navy was urged by Stalin personally, who overcame the opposition of high-ranking officers during the purges of 1937-8. The 59,150-ton, 28-knot battleship *Sovetskaya Ukraina* (seen on the slipway at the Marti Yard in Nikolayev in August 1941) was to be armed with three triple 406mm, six twin 152mm, eight 100mm AA, thirty-two 37mm AA and be protected by a 420mm belt. Of the planned four, three ships were laid down before the project was abandoned on 10 July 1941. (*Jerzy Micinski*)

▼5

6. The First World War vintage 29,150-ton British battleship *Royal Sovereign* was temporarily transferred to the Northern Fleet to satisfy the Russians' claim to a share of the surrendered Italian Navy. She is seen here flying Russian colours after the handing over ceremony on 30 May 1944 at Rosyth. Officially commissioned on 29 August 1944 at Polarnoe as *Arkhangelsk*, she was to be the largest ship in the battle fleet. She was returned on 4 February 1949 following the transfer of the ex-Italian battleship *Guilio Cesare* to the Black Sea Fleet. (Imperial War Museum, Neg No. A23814)

7. The 6,800-ton cruiser *Svetlana*, ordered in 1912 for the Baltic Fleet, was completed and commissioned in 1928 as *Profintern*. Transferred to the Black Sea in 1930, she was renamed once again in 1939 to become *Krasnyi Krym*. She is seen here exchanging fire with German shore artillery off Odessa in 1941. She was the most successful of the Russian cruisers, taking part in numerous actions but never suffering serious battle damage. In 1944 she was armed with fifteen 130mm, three twin 100mm AA, four 45mm AA, ten 37mm AA, seven 12.7mm machine-guns and two triple 456mm torpedo tubes. She could also carry 90 mines. Worn turbines limited her speed to 22 knots.

7▼

▲8　▼9

▼10

8. The cruiser *Admiral Lazarev* was laid down in 1913 for the Black Sea Fleet and was completed (to a modified design) and commissioned in 1932 as *Krasnyi Kavkaz*: 7,650 tons, 29 knots, the hull lengthened by six metres, two funnels instead of three, and experimental 180mm guns mounted in enclosed centreline turrets. She is seen here in 1945, armed with four 180mm, six twin 100mm AA, four 45mm AA, ten 37mm AA, two quadruple 12.7mm machine-guns, two triple 456mm torpedo tubes and rails for 100 mines. She was expended as a target during guided missile trials in the 1950s. (Boris Lemachko)

9. *Krasnyi Kavkaz* in 1942 at Sevastopol, taking civilian refugees aboard after having disembarked troops and munitions for the besieged city. Acting as a fast transport, she carried more than 25,000 men during the war.

10. *Kirov*, the prototype of the generation of classic Russian cruisers, seen in July 1944 engaging German positions from the commercial port at Leningrad.

11. *Voroshilov* was commissioned into the Black Sea Fleet in 1940, having incorporated minor improvements to the armour protection as compared with *Kirov*. This 1946 photograph shows the significant mixture of armament and controls: main guns and torpedoes of Italian design. Swedish automatic guns, British quadruple machine-guns as well as Type 279 and Type 285 radars, and German *Wackeltopf* director. (Boris Lemachko)

12. Action stations aboard *Voroshilov*. The triple 180mm guns were crowded into a common cradle, which indicates Italian influence on design. Such closely spaced barrels led to serious inaccuracies from shell interference when firing salvoes.

11▲   12▼

▲13 ▼14

▼15

13. The improved *Kirov*-class *Maxim Gorkiy* was commissioned into the Baltic Fleet in 1940. She is seen here ice-bound at Leningrad during the siege in the winter of 1943-4. She survived with her machinery intact, electricity being provided from ashore. Chimneys protrude upwards from scuttles forward, stoves having been fitted in the few habitable compartments. To deceive enemy observers, topmasts were removed, rangefinders hidden in a box-like awning and a low section of the hull was painted dark-grey as high as a pier.

14. *Molotov* was commissioned into the Black Sea Fleet one week before the German invasion; she is seen here when brand-new, with the KOR-1 type seaplane aboard. At the mainmast head she carried, though this is scarcely visible, the aerial of the Russian experimental shipborne warning radar Redut-K. (Boris Lemachko)

15. As a result of the Russo-German pact of 1939, the incomplete 16,900-ton *Hipper*-class heavy cruiser *Lützow* was sold to the Soviet Union. She was towed to Leningrad in May 1940 and when 70 per cent complete in June 1941 she was commissioned as the floating battery *Petropavlovsk* with two twin 203mm and twelve 37mm AA guns. Grounded on 17 September 1941 as result of German artillery fire (the wreck is seen here with a Russian explosives expert inspecting a German 210mm dud in the foreground), she was raised in 1942 and renamed *Tallin* the following year. In 1953 she became the stationary training ship *Dnepr* and was scrapped in 1959.

16 ▲

16. In 1944 the 7,000-ton US cruiser *Milwaukee* was temporarily transferred to the Russian Navy in lieu of part of the Russians' entitlement to surrendered Italian tonnage. She was commissioned into the Northern Fleet as *Murmansk* on 20 April 1944. Following the transfer of the ex-Italian cruiser *Duca d'Aosta* she was returned to the US Navy on 8 March 1949. She is seen here at Spithead still wearing Russian colours. (Maritime Photo Library)

17. Ten *Chapayev*-class cruisers of the 1938 Programme were initially planned as modified *Kirov*s, but with 152mm turrets. However, they were lengthened to accommodate the fourth turret and finally the 10,600-ton, 35-knots design was approved in 1939 with armament of four triple 152mm, eight 100mm AA, twelve 37mm AA, eight 12.7mm machine-guns and two quintuple 533mm torpedo tubes. Seven ships were actually laid down; two were captured by the Germans at Nikolayev and the remainder were completed post-war to an improved design. *Zheleznyakov* is seen late in her career. (Marek Twardowski)

17 ▼

18. Seventeen of the sixty-six turbine destroyers ordered for the Imperial Russian Navy from 1911 to 1917 formed the backbone of the Russian Navy's light forces by the late 1930s. All carried the names of Communist leaders. Of the seven Baltic Fleet ships, all were lost within the first three months of the war. *Lenin* (ex-*Kapitan Izylmetiev*), seen here in June 1941, was scuttled in Libau to avoid capture. (Marek Twardowski)

▲18 ▼19

19. The *Novik*-class *Karl Libknecht* (ex-*Kapitan Belli*) of the Northern Fleet in 1945. At that time she displaced more than 2,000 tons full load, could achieve 25 knots and was armed with four 102mm, two 76mm AA, two 45mm AA, two 37mm AA, two 20mm AA, three 12.7mm machine-guns, three triple 456mm torpedo tubes, two depth-charge throwers and 80 mines. (Marek Twardowski)

▼20

20. *Leningrad* (see in action at Leningrad in 1944) was the prototype of the class of six 2,150-ton flotilla leaders, the first destroyers to be laid down in Russia under the Soviet regime. Designated as substitute light cruisers, which the Russians lacked at that time, she was fast (42 knots) and strongly armed with five 130mm, two 76mm AA, six 37mm AA, six 12.7mm machine-guns, two quadruple 533mm torpedo tubes, two depth-charge throwers and 68 mines. Although impressive on paper they were not a success and the design was not developed.

21. A Type 7 destroyer of the Black Sea Fleet, her silhouette similar to that of the Italian *Oriani*-class ships. Of the total of fifty-four Type 7 and Type 7U destroyers laid down from 1934 to 1938, thirty were commissioned before the outbreak of war, while fifteen others entered service during hositilities. Eighteen of them were lost. (Marek Twardowski)

22. Dug during the first decade of the Soviet regime, at an enormous cost in slave labour, the 'Baltic-White Sea Canal' was used for the transfer of warships from the Baltic to the Arctic. *Gremyashchiy*, a Type 7, went this way to the Arctic following her completion at Leningrad. She is seen here in 1944, camouflaged and with the aerial of a British Type 286 surface radar visible at her foremast head. (Jerzy Micinski)

21▲ 22▼

23. In 1942 *Razyaryonnyi* was transferred to the Arctic from the Far East via the northern sea route. She entered service in European waters, because of the time needed to transport the material to Komsomolsk, but profited from the delay by receiving modified weapons (compare her guns with those of *Gremyashchiy*). (Imperial War Museum, Neg No. A22471)

24. The Type 7 destroyer *Gremyashchiy* seen in late 1944 leading another of her class and two *Novik*-class destroyers escorted by *MO4*-class sub-chasers. (Jerzy Micinski)

25. The 1,990-ton, 35-knot Type 7U destroyer *Silnyi* of the Baltic Fleet was armed with four 130mm, three 76mm AA, seven 37mm AA, eight 13.7mm machine-guns, three triple 533mm torpedo tubes, two depth-charge throwers and could carry 58 mines. The third 76mm AA gun seen abaft the 130mm 'D' mounting was not a typical feature of the class. (Boris Lemachko)

26. The stern of this Black Sea Fleet Type 7U destroyer is much less crowded with anti-submarine weapons than its British counterpart. Only two BMB 1 type depth-charge throwers and a pair of rails were fitted, with capacity for ten 135kg and twenty 25kg charges.

25 ▲ 26 ▼

27. The wreck of *Svobodnyi* photographed by an Italian on 16 July 1942, ten days after the Germans captured Sevastopol. Note the extent of the damage caused by nine bombs which hit the ship. (Aldo Fraccaroli)

27 ▼

28. *Slavnyi* of the Baltic Fleet, after the war. (Boris Lemachko)

29. The experimental 1,570-ton destroyer *Opytnyi*, was built to test an all-welded hull and high-pressure Ramsin boiler design. After failing speed trials in 1940, when 35 knots were achieved against the 43 knots anticipated, she was provisionally armed with three single 130mm, four 45mm AA, three 37mm AA, two quadruple 533mm torpedo tubes and served as a floating battery at Leningrad. Experiments were continued after the war. (Boris Lemachko)

30. The 3,200-ton, 44-knot flotilla leader *Tashkent* was ordered in 1935 from Italy to enhance Russian design practice. She is seen here in the summer of 1941 with three twin 130mm, six 37mm AA, six 12.7mm machine-guns, three triple 533mm torpedo tubes and rails fitted for 80 mines.

31. Of the twenty 2,240-ton, 37-knot *Ognevoi*-class destroyers laid down prior to the war, only one had been commissioned by 1945 and just eleven others by 1949. They were to be armed with two twin 130mm, two 76mm AA, three 37mm AA, four 12.7mm machine-guns, two triple 533mm torpedo tubes, two depth-charge throwers and 96 mines. To avoid their capture

▲28 ▼29

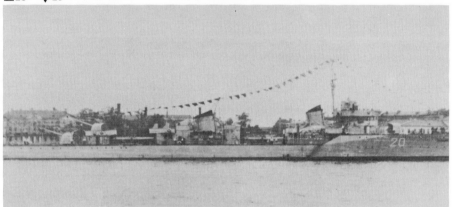

▼30

by the advancing Germans, some of the incomplete hulls were evacuated – *Ozornoi* is seen here at the small Caucasian port of Batum. (Boris Lemachko)

32. A squadron force consisting of the First World War vintage 29,150-ton British battleship *Royal Sovereign* (commissioned by the Russians as *Arkhangelsk*), eight *Town*-class destroyers and four modern submarines seen assembled at Rosyth on 30 May 1944 awaiting handing-over to the Northern Fleet to satisfy the Russians' claim to a share of the surrendered Italian Navy. All of these ships, with the exception of the ones lost in action, were returned from 1949 to 1952 following the transfer of the ex-Italian vessels. (Imperial War Museum, Neg. No. A23786)

31▲   32▼

▲ 33   ▼ 34

33. The Russians took every opportunity to enlarge their naval forces with booty regardless of quality or origin. Even Roumania's defection to the Allied cause in September 1944 did not prevent the seizure of her tiny fleet of four destroyers (*Regele Ferdinand* seen here as Russian *Likhoi*), three submarines, five motor boats and five river monitors. (Boris Lemachko)

34. The six *D* Class 941/1,288-ton, 14/8.7-knot 'Series I' boats of the 1926 Programme were the first submarines designed under the Soviet regime. Although heavily armed with eight 533mm torpedo tubes, single 100mm and 45mm AA guns, they were of inferior quality because of design faults. *D3* (*Krasnogvardeyec* of the Northern Fleet is seen here after her 1938–40 reconstruction which included remodelling of the conning tower and addition of sheer. She was lost in July 1942 off the coast of Norway. (Imperial War Museum, Neg No. RUS4539)

35. The design of the *L* Class submarines was modelled on the British *L55*, sunk in 1919 and raised by the Russians in 1928. Following the laying down of six 'Series II' and 'Series XI' boats (1,025/1,321 tons, 14/8.5 knots, six bow 533mm torpedo tubes, single 100mm and 45mm AA guns, twenty mines in two horizontal stern tubes), the design was modified to the 'Series XIII' (seen here) in 1934. Enlarged by 75tons, she had two stern 533mm torpedo tubes added and high-power diesels were fitted in order to attain 17 knots on the surface. By 1959, seven boats had been built with five others of the 'Series XIIIbis' by 1943. (Imperial War Museum, Neg No. RUS4404)

36. *L15* entering the US submarine base at Coco Solo in the Panama Canal Zone on 21 October 1942. With her sister *L16* they were earmarked for transfer from the Far East to the Arctic; but the operation, which began on 25 September 1942, was not a success; on 11 October 1942 *L16* was torpedoed and sunk by the Japanese submarine *I25*, 600 miles off the Oregon coast. *L15* arrived at Polarnoe on 23 May 1943 well illustrating the isolation of the Russian naval forces from various areas. (Official US Navy Photo)

37. The Baltic Fleet *Shch303 (Ersh)*, seen in 1943. She was one of the original four 'Series III' boats that formed the *Shchuka* class. These 572/700-ton, 11.8/8-knot submarines were built from 1930 to 1934 and were armed with six 533mm torpedo tubes and one 45mm AA gun. Two of her sister ships were lost when trying to penetrate the German-Finish blockade in the Gulf of Finland from June to December 1942. Three groups of submarines, totalling 37 boats, made repeated attempts to force their way out into the Baltic; the resultant campaign in the Baltic led to the sinking of 23 enemy ships and a further eight damaged (total 84,000 GRT) at a cost of fourteen Russian vessels.

35▲ 36▼

37▼

38. In 1930 the *Shch* class was modified by lengthening the hull by 1.5 metres, the compartmentation was changed and one 45mm AA gun was added aft of the conning tower. From 1931 to 1935 39 boats were built, consisting of the 'Series V', 'V-bis' (seen here) and 'Vbis-2' designs. (Imperial War Museum, Neg No. RUS979)

▲38   ▼39

39. The 'Series X' *Shch209* of the Black Sea Fleet with experimental net cutters at the bow. (Imperial War Museum, Neg No. RUS2245)

▼40

40. A *Shch*-class 'Series Vbis' submarine of the Black Sea Fleet landing frogmen behind enemy lines.

41. Hoisting a 53-38U-type 533mm torpedo aboard the 'Series X' *Shch215* of the Black Sea Fleet in 1943. During the war Russian submarines undertook 679 attacks expending 1,550 torpedoes which resulted in 28 (33 according to Russian sources) warships and 108 (157) merchantmen of 254,525GRT)(462,313GRT) being sunk at the cost of at least 89 submarines lost, many with all hands. Total war losses amounted to at least 108 boats.

42. Twenty-eight of the thirty 'Series VI' *M*-class boats, built at the Ural Machine Works, were transported by rail to Vladivostok after running trials in the Black Sea. The design had been modified to improve hydrodynamic qualities, and twenty 'Series VIbis' (seen here) boats were ordered. These single-shaft boats of 160/196 tons and 13/7 knots were armed with two bow 533mm torpedo tubes and one 45mm AA gun. (Aldo Fraccaroli)

41▲ 42▼

SOVIET FLEETS AND FLOTILLAS 1941–1945

Unit	Formed	Disbanded	Main Base	C-in-C
Baltic Fleet	11 Feb 1918	—	Tallin Kronshtadt, Sept 1941 Leningrad, Oct 1941 Kronshtadt, June 1942 Leningrad, Jan 1943 Kronshtadt, June 1944 Tallin, Oct 1944	Adm V. F. Tributs
Northern Fleet	1 June 1933	—	Polarnoe	Rear-Adm A. G. Golovko
Black Sea Fleet	March 1920	—	Sevastopol Poti, July 1942 Sevastopol, Oct 1944	Vice-Adm F. S. Oktyabrskij Vice-Adm L. A. Valdimirskij, 24 Apr 1943 Vice-Adm N. E. Basistyj, 10 March 1944 Vice-Adm F. S. Oktyabrskij, 28 March 1944
Pacific Fleet	21 Apr 1932	—	Vladivostok	Vice-Adm I. S. Yumashev
Amur Flotilla	May 1920	c.1950	Khabarovsk	Rear-Adm P. S. Aban'kin Vice-Adm F. S. Oktyabrskij, 29 June 1943 Rear-Adm P. S. Aban'kin, 21 March 1944 Rear-Adm F. S. Sedel'nikov, 2 Sept 1944 Rear-Adm N. V. Antonov, 23 June 1945
Azov Flotilla	25 July 1942	14 Oct 1942	Mariupol Primorsko-Akhtarsk, Oct 1941	Commodore A. P. Aleksandrov Rear-Adm S. G. Gorshkov, 13 Oct 1941
	20 Feb 1943	20 Apr 1944	Ejsk Primorsko-Akhtarsk, Sept 1943 Temryuk, Apr 1944	Rear-Adm G. N. Kholostyakov, 5 Jan 1944 Rear-Adm S. G. Gorshkov, 6 Jan 1944
Caspian Flotilla	5 July 1920	—	Baku	Rear-Adm F. S. Sedel'nikov Rear-Adm F. V. Zozulya
Chudskaya Flotilla	June 1941	13 Aug 1941	Gdov	Commodore N. Yu Avraamov
Dnieper Flotilla	22 Sept 1943	Dec 1945	Chernigov Kiev, Nov 1943 Pinsk, July 1944	Commodore V. V. Grigor'ev
Danube Flotilla	28 June 1940	21 Nov 1941	Izmail Nikolaev, Oct 1941	Rear-Adm N. O. Abramov Rear-Adm A. S. Frolov, 16 Sept 1941
	20 Apr 1944	1945	Odessa Izmail, Aug 1944	Rear-Adm S. G. Gorshkov Rear-Adm G. N. Kholostyakov, 12 Dec 1944
Ilmen Flotilla	28 July 1941	20 Oct 1941	Novgorod	Commander V. M. Drevnitskij
Ladoga Flotilla	18 June 1941	4 Nov 1944	Schlusselbourg Novaya Ladoga, Sept 1941	Captain V. P. Baranovskij Captain S. V. Zemlyniachenko, 30 June 1941 Commodore V. P. Bogolepov, 24 July 1941 Commodore B. V. Khoroshkhin, 8 Aug 1941 Commodore V. C. Cherokov, 13 Oct 1944
Northern Pacific Flotilla	Aug 1939	1945	Sovetskaya Gavan'	Rear-Adm M. I. Arapov Rear-Adm V. A. Andreev
Onega Flotilla	7 Aug 1941	28 Nov 1941	Petrozavodsk Voznesen'e, Aug 1941 Vyterga, Oct 1941	Commodore A. P. D'yakonov
	13 Dec 1942	10 July 1944	Vyterga	Commadore A. P. D'yakonov Commodore N. V. Antonov, 7 July 1943 Rear-Adm P. S. Aban'kin, 11 Aug 1943 Commodore N. V. Antonov, 7 Jan 1944

Unit	Formed	Disbanded	Main Base	C-in-C
Pinsk Flotilla	23 June 1940	5 Oct 1941	Pinsk Kiev, July 1941	Rear-Adm D. D. Rogachev
White Sea Flotilla	15 Aug 1941	15 Apr 1945	Arkhangelsk	Rear-Adm M. M. Dolinin Rear-Adm G. A. Stepanov, 7 Oct 1941 Rear-Adm S. G. Kucherov, 11 March 1943 Vice-Adm Yu. A. Panteleev, 30 Aug 1944
Volga Flotilla	28 Oct 1941	30 June 1944	Ul'yanovsk	Commodore S. G. Sapozhnikov Rear-Adm S. M. Vorob'eb, 6 Nov 1941 Rear-Adm D. D. Rogachev, 16 Feb 1942 Rear-Adm Yu. A. Panteleev, 14 May 1943 Commodore P. A. Smirinov, 16 Dec 1943

SEVASTOPOL

ex-*Parizhskaya Kommuna*, from 31 May 1943
ex-*Sevastopol*, from 31 March 1921

Type	Lineynyj korabl' Battleship
Class	*Gangut*; from 1931 *Marat*
Builder	Baltic Yard, St Petersburg
Laid down	16 June 1909
Launched	29 June 1911
Commissioned	17 Nov 1914
Data valid for	1944
Deployment	Black Sea Fleet
Displacement	30,395t normal, 31,275t full load
Dimensions	184.5m oa × 32.5m × 9.7m max.
Armament	four triple 305mm, sixteen 120mm, six 76mm AA, sixteen 37mm AA, fourteen 12.7mm MG
Armour (max.)	belt 230mm, decks 150mm, turrets 250mm
Electronics	none
Machinery	Twenty-two Yarrow boilers, 4-shaft Parsons turbines, 61,000bhp
Speed	21.5kts
Endurance	2,500nm at 14kts
Complement	1,546 officers & men
Fate	sold for scrap 17 Feb 1956

The four *Gangut*-class dreadnoughts were the first to be built in Russia after the Russo-Japanese War. Following their completion in December 1914 they were deployed with the Baltic Fleet and after a period of inactivity during the war they were demobilized in January 1918. *Sevastopol* returned to service in 1921 under the name of *Parizhskaya*

STRENGTH OF THE SOVIET NAVY 1941/1945

	Baltic Fleet		Black Sea Fleet		Northern Fleet		Pacific Fleet	
	22 June 1941	1 Jan 1945	22 June 1941	May 1944	22 June 1941	1 Jan 1945	22 June 1941	10 Aug 1945
Battleships	2	1	1	1	—	1	—	—
Cruisers	2	2	5	4	—	1	—	2
Flotilla Leaders	2	2	3	—	—	1	2	1
Destroyers	17	10	14	6	8	17	5	12
Submarines	71	28	44	29	15	22	85	78
Escort Vessels	7	5	2	13	7	12	6	19
Gunboats	2	10	4	3	—	—	—	—
Minesweepers	30	73	12	27	2	36	18	52
Motor Torpedo-Boats	67	78	78	47	—	40	145	204
Patrol Boats	33	220	24	113	14	59	19	49
Aircraft	656	781	625	467	116	721	500	1618

Kommuna. Transferred to the Black Sea in 1930, to keep the balance with Turkey, she underwent thorough reconstruction from 1933 to 1938 which featured additions to the forecastle and bulges, introduction of fire control systems and oil-fired boilers, increase of AA defence, deck armour and elevation of 12in guns. Following the outbreak of the Second World War, she was based at Sevastopol (the main base of the Black Sea Fleet), but in October 1941 was evacuated eastwards to avoid enemy air attacks. Involved in coastal bombardment duty during the defence of the Crimea in the winter of 1941/2, she was withdrawn to Poti in March 1942 for repairs, but remained there until hostilities ended in the Black Sea. Reverting to her original name in 1943, she was again based at Sevastopol on 5 November 1944 and the following year was decorated for exceptional(!) war activity.

KIROV

Type	Legkij krejser Light cruiser
Class	*Kirov*
Builder	Ordzhonikidze Yard, Leningrad
Laid down	22 Oct 1935
Launched	30 Nov 1936
Commissioned	23 Sept 1938
Data valid for	1944
Deployment	Baltic Fleet
Displacement	7,880t standard, 9,436t full load
Dimensions	191.0m oa × 17.66m × 6.15m max.
Armament	three triple 180mm, eight 100mm AA, ten 37mm AA, four 12.7mm MG, two triple 533mm torpedo tubes, four depth-charge throwers, 100 mines

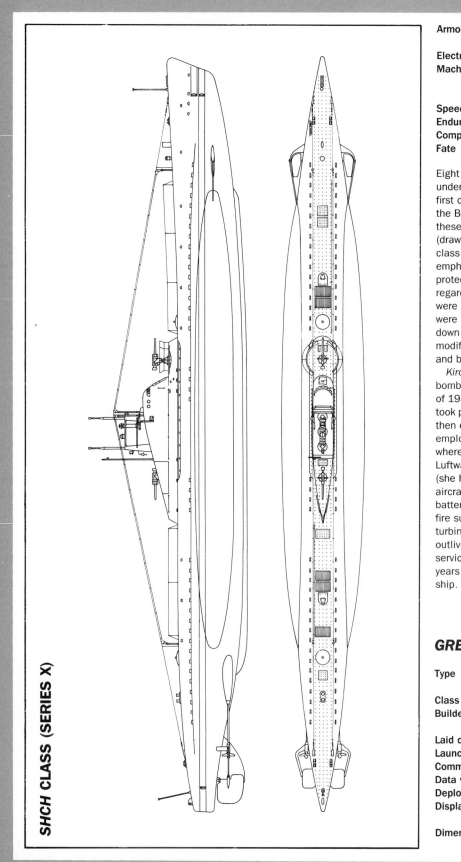

SHCH CLASS (SERIES X)

Armour (max.)	belt 70mm, deck 50mm, turrets 100mm
Electronics	warning radar
Machinery	Six Yarrow boilers 2-shaft Parsons geared turbines, 113,000bhp
Speed	35.94kts
Endurance	3,750nm at 18kts
Complement	872 officers & men
Fate	deleted 1974

Eight *Kirov*-class cruisers, authorized under the 1933 Programme, were the first cruisers to be built in Russia after the Bolshevik Revolution. Design of these ships was based on Italian practice (drawings of the *Raimondo Montecuccoli* class had been provided) and therefore emphasized speed over inadequate protection, although hull scantlings, regarded by the Russian as too light, were strengthened (200 tons of steel were added). Only two ships were laid down to the original design which was modified in 1936 to improve protection and bridge structure.

  Kirov was employed for shore bombardment duty during the Winter War of 1939/40 against Finland. In 1941 she took part in the defence of Tallin and was then evacuated to Kronstadt and employed in the defence of Leningrad where she was damaged twice by the Luftwaffe. Operational again in 1943 (she had surrendered her catapult and aircraft by that time to improve her AA battery), *Kirov* was employed later as a fire support ship in Leningrad. Having turbines of Italian manufacture she outlived her sisters and remained in service until 1974, seeing out her last years as a headquarters and training ship.

GREMYASHCHIJ

Type	Eskadrennyj minonosec Fleet torpedo boat
Class	*Gnevnyj*
Builder	Zhdanov Yard, Leningrad
Laid down	23 July 1936
Launched	18 March 1937
Commissioned	28 Aug 1939
Data valid for	1944
Deployment	Northern Fleet
Displacement	1,885t standard, 2,402t full load
Dimensions	112.5m oa × 10.2m × 4.1m max.

Armament	four 130mm, two 76mm AA, four 37mm AA, four 12.7mm MG, two triple 533mm torpedo tubes, two depth-charge throwers, 56 mines
Electronics	British Type-286 surface warning radar British Asdic
Machinery	Three watertube boilers, 2-shaft geared turbines, 48,000shp
Speed	37kts
Endurance	2,720nm at 19kts
Complement	246 officers & men
Fate	deleted 1956

The 1933 Programme provided for the construction of destroyers for the first time in the Soviet Union. The Russians, lacking the necessary experience, sought the design assistance of the Ansaldo shipyard. The new destroyers thus resembled the Italian single-funnelled boats, but as a result they incorporated faults inherent in this design — structural weakness and limited seaworthiness. The latter was caused by the armament and fittings which were heavier than those of Italian manufacture; so fully loaded were the Russian boats that they drew almost 700 tons in excess of the original design. In May 1937 the design was improved to strengthen the hull and to remodel the machinery layout by alternating the arrangement of the boiler and turbine rooms, which resulted in changes to the two-funnelled silhouette.

In September 1939 *Gremyashchij* was transferred from the Baltic to the White Sea via the Stalin Canal. She was one of the most successful Russian warships of the war; operating in an extremely difficult environment she accomplished ninety war missions, sixty convoys and provided fire support for ten landing operations. According to Russian sources she sank the German submarine *U585* and shot down fourteen aircraft.

M172

ex-M88, from 16 June 1939

Type	Malaya podvodnaya lodka Small submarine boat
Class	M
Builder	Sudomekh Works, Leningrad
Laid down	17 June 1936
Launched	12 June 1937
Commissioned	11 Dec 1937
Data valid for	1941
Deployment	Northern Fleet
Displacement	206t surfaced, 258t submerged
Dimensions	44.5m × 3.3m × 3.0m
Armament	two bow 533mm torpedo tubes, one 45mm AA, two 7.6mm MG
Electronics	Mars-type hydrophones
Machinery	2-shaft diesel engine + electric motor, 800bhp surfaced, 400shp submerged
Speed	13.2kts surfaced, 8.2kts submerged
Endurance	3,600nm at 8.5kts surfaced, 90nm at 3kts submerged
Complement	22 officers & men
Fate	lost Oct 1943, Barents Sea, probably mined

The *M* class coastal submarines were the result of a demand during the early 1930s for a boat that could be built by mass-production methods at an inland works and transported to the coast by rail. In the interests of simplicity, fighting and navigational qualities had to be sacrificed to a considerable degree, the extent of which became obvious following trials of the prototypes. In 1934, to remedy the more serious shortcomings, the design was modified and orders were shifted to the experienced naval yards at Leningrad and Nikolaev so as to achieve better standards of construction. However, satisfactory results were obtained only after the 'Series XII' design had been introduced in 1936. A total of twenty-eight boats of the latter type were completed before the war, and a further seventeen had been built by 1944.

In May 1939, *M88*, following a training period in the Baltic, was renumbered *M172* and transferred to the Arctic via the Stalin Canal. She carried out eighteen patrols before she was lost (probably mined), and was credited by the Russians with nine 'hits', of which number only the sinking of one transport and one patrol boat were confirmed after the war.

SHCH402

ex-*SHCH314*, from 16 May 1937

Type	Srednyaya podvodnaya lodka Medium submarine boat
Class	*Shchuka*
Builder	Ordzhonikidze Yard, Leningrad
Laid down	4 Dec 1934
Launched	28 June 1935
Commissioned	23 Sept 1936
Data valid for	1941
Deployment	Northern Fleet
Displacement	590t surfaced, 708t submerged
Dimensions	58.75m × 6.2m × 4.3m
Armament	four bow and two aft 533mm torpedo tubes, two 45mm AA, two 7.6mm MG
Electronics	Mars-type hydrophones
Machinery	two 2-shaft diesel engines + electric motors, 1,600bhp surfaced, 800shp submerged
Speed	13.6kts surfaced, 8.7kts submerged
Endurance	4,500nm at 8.9kts surfaced, 100nm at 2.5kts submerged
Complement	40 officers & men
Fate	sunk 21 Sept 1944, Barents Sea, accidentally by Soviet aircraft

The *Shchuka*-class medium submarines were developed during the late 1920s from the Dutch *AG* class built for the Imperial Russian Navy. In 1934 the design was remodelled to the 'Series X' which accommodated technical innovations obtained from the Germans. Thirty-two boats of this type were completed before the war with a further nine of the improved 'Series Xbis' being completed in 1941 and a final eight commissioned post-war.

SHCH314, following training with the Baltic Fleet, was renumbered *SHCH402* and transferred to the Arctic in June 1937. During the winter of 1937/8 she took part in the rescue of the drifting polar ship *Severnyj Polyus*. In contrast to her rather dull patrol service during the Winter War against Finland, her Great Patriotic War service was as adventurous as it was ineffectual. During sixteen war missions she actually sank three ships, although she claimed nine plus a *U-boat*. She twice missed destruction by a hairsbreadth, being severely disabled by German patrols in March 1942, and then damaged by a hydrogen explosion six months later.

METEL'

Type	Storozhevoj korabl' Guard ship
Class	*Uragan*
Builder	Zhdanov Yard, Leningrad (construction) Dalzavod Works, Vladivostok (assembly)
Laid down	18 Dec 1931
Launched	15 June 1934 (at Vladivostok)
Commissioned	18 Nov 1934
Data valid for	1944
Deployment	Pacific Fleet
Displacement	450t standard, 619t full load
Dimensions	71.5m oa × 7.4m × 2.6m max.
Armament	two 102mm, three 37mm AA, three 12.7mm MG, one triple 456mm torpedo tubes, two depth-charge throwers, 30 mines
Electronics	Posejdon-type hydrophones
Machinery	two 3-drum watertube boilers, 2-shaft geared turbines, 6,290shp
Speed	23kts
Endurance	1,500nm at 14kts
Complement	108 officers & men
Fate	training ship since Oct 1945

Eighteen of the *Uragan*-class guard ships were authorized under the 1926 Programme to replace the old torpedo-boats hitherto used for coastal patrol duties. They were the first surface warships built in Russia under the Soviet regime, a process which involved numerous difficulties ranging from shortage of experienced naval architects, engineers and skilled workmen to deficiency in technology and the low quality of industrial products. It was small wonder that they inherited the worst traditions of Russian shipbuilding being topheavy, overweight and underpowered. They attained 23kts on trials, although 29kts had been anticipated.

Metel', albeit destined for the Pacific Fleet, was built in Leningrad and after the completion of her hull in 1933 she was dismantled and transported in sections to Vladivostok by the Trans-Siberian Railway. There she was reassembled, launched and finally completed. In July–August 1938, during the Russo-Japanese conflict, *Metel'* screened troop convoys off Chasan Lake. After war was declared on Japan in August 1945, she took part in assaults on the east coast of Korea, landing troops and shelling enemy positions.

MOTOR TORPEDO BOAT 106

'MOSKOVSKIJ REMESLENNIK TRUDOVYKH REZERVOV'
No *TK412* from 23 Feb 1944

Type	Vooruzhennyj kater Armed boat
Class	G5
Builder	Zelenodolsk Yard, River Volga
Laid down	1941
Launched	April 1942
Commissioned	5 May 1943
Data valid for	1943
Deployment	Black Sea Fleet
Displacement	16.26t full load
Dimensions	19.1m oa × 3.4m × 0.8m max.
Armament	launcher for twenty-four 82mm rockets, two 12.7mm MG
Electronics	none
Machinery	2-shaft Packard 4M-2500 petrol engines, 2,400bhp
Speed	50kts
Endurance	220nm
Complement	2 officers & 5 men
Fate	deleted 1950s

Design of the G5-class motor torpedo-boats was developed from the British *CMBs*, a few of which remained in Soviet hands after the Civil War. The prototype, albeit with an aluminium alloy hull instead of double mahogany as in the British boats, ran trials in 1927 and series production began under the designation *SH4*. In 1933 the design was recast to the G5 class with 21in torpedoes replacing the 18in, and engines of local production were introduced. Some 329 boats were built to this design from 1934–1944, divided into five basic series. In 1942, following the successful use of home-made Katyusha 88mm rocket-launchers from boats of this type, the naval authorities ordered 82mm and 132mm army rocket-launchers to be adapted for naval use (242 had been ordered by 1945). Some of the G5-class boats completed from 1943 to 1944 had torpedo wells plated out, and missile-launchers mounted above the conning tower.

Funds to complete *No. 106* were raised by public subscription so, in addition to her number, she bore the name commemorating the donors (Moscow artisans). She participated in landings on Kerch in November 1943 and in the Crimea in April 1944. From April 1945 she served with the Danube Flotilla.

MOTOR TORPEDO BOAT 14

Type	Torpednyj kater Torpedo-boat
Class	D3
Builder	Shipyard No 25, Leningrad
Laid down	1939
Launched	1940
Commissioned	22 July 1941
Data valid for	1941
Deployment	Northern Fleet
Displacement	32.1t full load
Dimensions	21.6m oa × 3.9m × 1.35m max.
Armament	two 533mm torpedo tubes/launching gears, two 12.7mm MG, eight depth-charges
Electronics	Tsefej-type hydrophones
Machinery	3-shaft GAM-34F petrol engines, 3,150bhp
Speed	37kts
Endurance	550nm at 8kts
Complement	2 officers & 6–8 men
Fate	sunk 15 Sept 1944 off North Cape by German surface craft

Since the mid-1930s the Soviet Navy had run an experimental programme with a view to producing large, seaworthy motor torpedo-boats. Following trials of the G5-derived boats of various sizes, the stern-launching system was abandoned in favour of deck torpedo-launching racks. Soon two types of wooden- and steel-hulled boats of this kind were selected for further evaluation. The general performance of the larger, wooden-hulled boat was found to be satisfactory and series production began in 1939 under the designation D3 class. Because of engine shortages fifty-six hulls were completed as subchasers and it was only when Packard engines became available that the construction programme reached its peak. A total of 119 boats, (torpedo-boats or subchasers) had been built by 1944.

Following trials in the Baltic during the summer of 1941, under the designation *Letayushchij 5*, she was transferred by railway to the Arctic to be commissioned on 16 August 1941 as *No. 14*. She took part in actions against German traffic off the north Norwegian coast and claimed two hits on coastal ships (neither confirmed). She was sunk by German patrol craft of 61 Vorposten during an attack on the Petsamo-Kirkenes convoy.

PATROL LAUNCH *SKA 065*

M065 from 7 May 1944
ex-*SKA No. 124*, from 17 Dec 1942
ex-*PK125*, from 10 Dec 1941

Type	Malyj okhotnik Small hunter
Class	*MO4*
Builder	inland yard
Laid down	1938
Launched	1938
Commissioned	1938
Data valid for	1943
Deployment	Black Sea Fleet
Displacement	50.5t standard, 56.5t full load
Dimensions	26.9m oa × 4.0m × 1.5m max.
Armament	two 45mm AA, two 12.7mm, three 7.6mm MG, thirty-two depth-charges, four mines
Electronics	Posejdon-type hydrophones
Machinery	3-shaft GAM-34BS petrol engines, 2,550bhp
Speed	26kts
Endurance	470nm at 7kts
Complement	24 officers & men
Fate	probably deleted mid-1950s

The consolidation of Stalin's totalitarian regime during the early 1930s required closely sealed sea borders to guard against either foreign infiltration or Russian citizens trying to leave. Such political imperatives necessitated the development of coastal forces which could also be used for patrol and anti-submarine duties in the event of war. This force was to be built around *MO2*-class wooden-hulled motor launches developed as a joint venture of the *NKVD* and the Russian Navy. Following completion of the first batch of 27 boats in 1936, the design was abandoned and replaced in 1937 by the improved *MO4* class. Some 219 boats had been

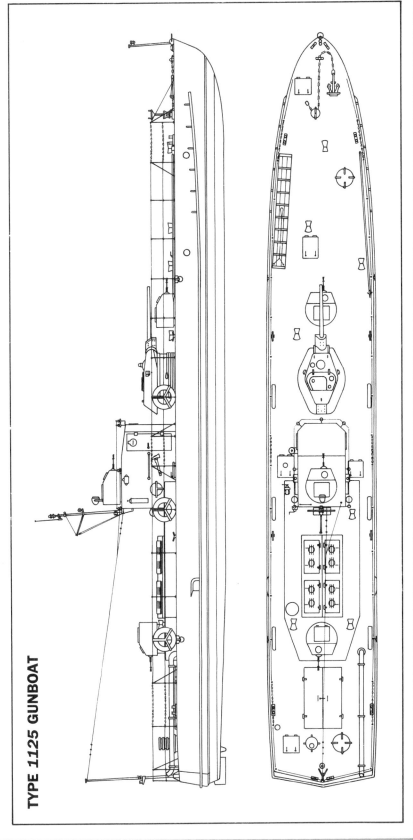

TYPE 1125 GUNBOAT

completed by 1943 when production of this type was terminated.

SKA065 entered service as the patrol boat of the 1st Division of the Black Sea NKVD Frontier Guard, and was commissioned with the Black Sea Fleet on 19 July 1941. She took part in defence actions off Odessa, Sevastopol and along the Caucasian coast, then later participated in the recapture of the Crimea. According to official records she covered 30,000 miles, escorted 250 convoys and repulsed more than 300 air attacks during the course of the war.

MOTOR LAUNCH SK503

Type	Bronirovannyj malyj okhotnki Armoured small hunter
Class	BMO
Builder	Zhdanov Yard, Leningrad
Laid down	Autumn 1942
Launched	Spring 1943
Commissioned	30 June 1943
Data valid for	1943
Deployment	Baltic Fleet
Displacement	62t full load
Dimensions	24.75m oa × 4.2m × 1.6m max.
Armament	one 45mm AA, one 37mm AA, two twin 12.7mm MG, eight depth-charges, ten mines
Armour (max)	belt, fuel tanks and bridge 10—12mm
Electronics	Drakon-type sonar
Machinery	2-shaft Packard petrol engines, 2,400bhp, 1-shaft Continental petrol engine, 80bhp
Speed	23kts
Endurance	? (6t of petrol)
Complement	26 officers & men
Fate	mined 5 July 1944, Gulf of Finland

Experiences in combat with the MO4-class motor launches resulted in a request from the Chief of the Baltic Fleet in July 1942 for the design and construction of an armoured patrol/anti-submarine boat. Besides armour plates distributed along the waterline, around fuel tanks, magazines and the conning tower, tight compartmentation was also stressed. Although the programme, designated BMO class, got as high a priority as was possible in besieged

Leningrad, construction and trials of the prototype lasted until May 1943 (she remained idle during four months of the 1942/3 winter because of ice). Facilities for series manufacture were created: the boats were built in two sections on direct production lines — to cope with an order for 66 launches. In the event only 48 boats were commissioned, at a rate of three per month, before the end of hostilities. Ten of these were lost.

SK503 was mined of Teikarsaari Island in action against the futile attempts of German-Finnish forces to support an isolated garrison there.

ARMOURED GUNBOAT BK140

Type	Bronekater Armoured boat
Class	BK-1125-III
Builder	Rechsudoverf Yard at Perm, River Kama
Laid down	1944
Launched	Summer 1944
Commissioned	13 March 1945
Data valid for	1945
Deployment	Dnieper Flotilla
Displacement	26t standard, 29.3t full load
Dimensions	22.65m oa × 3.55m × 0.56m mean
Armament	one 76mm gun in T34-type tank turret, two twin 12.7mm, one 6.7mm MG
Armour (max)	belt, bridge, turret 4—7mm
Electronics	none
Machinery	1-shaft GAM-34B petrol engine, 850bhp
Speed	18kts
Endurance	180nm
Complement	10 officers & men
Fate	preserved at Perm since 1974

In the vast land areas of Russia, the rivers and lakes were the best and most reliable means of communication and defence. Utilising positive experience of this type of warfare gained during the Civil War, the Russians worked on designs of river gunboats such as had been built for the Imperial Russian Navy. By 1935 they had developed two basic types of river armoured gunboats armed either with two (1124 Type) or one (1125 Type) 3in guns mounted in tank turrets. After the turret of the T-34-type medium

tank became available in 1939, most of the new gunboats received it.

By the time of the German invasion some 70 gunboats had been commissioned and 85 were under construction. They were followed by an order for 100 in August 1941 which was completed by the end of 1945. About 90 of these were lost.

BK140 only reached the main body of the Dnieper Flotilla on 12 April 1945, having been operating on the River Spree in support of the army during the final struggle for Berlin. After the war she was transferred to the Far East and was finally sold for scrap in the late 1960s. Recovered from the breakers at Khabarovsk, she is preserved as an onshore memorial at Perm.

MINESWEEPER T404

Type	Bazovyj Tral'shchik Base minesweeper
Class	FUGAS
Builder	Sevastopol Naval Yard
Laid down	Autumn 1934
Launched	10 Dec 1936
Commissioned	30 Oct 1937
Data valid for	1944
Deployment	Black Sea Fleet
Displacement	433t standard, 494t full load
Dimensions	62.0m oa × 7.6m × 2.4m max.
Armament	one 100mm AA, one 45mm AA, three 37mm AA, three 12.7mm MG, twenty depth-charges, twenty-seven mines
Electronics	none
Machinery	2-shaft diesel engines, 2,800bhp
Speed	18.5kts
Endurance	3,400nm at 14kts
Complement	66 officers & men
Fate	deleted 1950s

The diesel-powered Fugas class medium minesweepers were intended to be the standard type under the second and third Five-Year Plans. Of 48 hulls laid down prior to the German invasion, forty had been commissioned by the end of 1945 (half of this number were lost in action) with a further four probably finished afterwards. They were sturdy, strongly armed, fitted for minelaying and fast enough to serve as escorts. The power plant of the first series boats presented problems with speed control (maintaining low speeds especially) which excluded the possibility of pair sweeping; besides this fundamental fault the main sweep winch was underpowered. They were also criticized for insufficient stability and inadequate storage of fresh water. Most of these difficulties were subsequently overcome on the boats laid down after 1936.

Shchit (she received her number designation in July 1939) took part in the defence of Odessa and Sevastopol and was damaged by coastal batteries on 29 December 1941 during an assault on the Crimea. Afterwards she acted along the Caucasian coast and later participated in landings off Novorossisk in February 1943 and Varna in September 1944.

MINESWEEPER *T467*

Type	Malyj Tral'shchik Small minesweeper
Class	*T351*
Builder	Leningrad
Laid down	Spring 1945
Launched	Autumn 1945
Commissioned	Winter 1945
Data valid for	1945
Deployment	Baltic Fleet
Displacement	145.8t standard, 160.4t full load
Dimensions	38.0m oa × 5.7m × 1.5m
Armament	two 45mm AA, two twin 12.7mm MG, twelve depth-charges, twelve mines
Electronics	Tamir-10-type Sonar

Machinery	3-shaft, Superior diesel engines 1,440bhp
Speed	11.7kts
Endurance	2,400nm
Complement	25 officers & men
Fate	transferred to the Polish Navy, 5 Apr 1946

Work on a mass production programme of expendable, shallow draught, steel coastal minesweepers had started immediately following the outbreak of war. Orders were placed in Leningrad, but the design required modifications to ensure simplicity of construction and economic use of materials. Straight hull lines were adopted so that flat sections could be used throughout, thus saving manpower, The power plant was built around Lend-Lease supplied engines and after successful trials of the prototype boat series production began in spring of 1943. The design was modernized in 1944: the hull was lengthened, engines were placed in separate rooms, machine-guns doubled and fuel capacity tripled. Thirty-nine boats had been commissioned with the Baltic Fleet when hostilities ended. These had been followed by another 53 by the end of 1945. Production was continued at Rybinsk and lasted until 1956. The Class finally totalled more than 260 vessels and 44 of them were sold to satellite navies.

T476 was transferred to the Polish Navy on 5 April 1946 as its quota of the surrendered German Navy, and was commissioned as *Orlik*.

TENDER *No 24*

Type	Tender
Class	*15–ton*
Builder	Pertozavod Works, Leningrad
Laid down	Summer 1942
Launched	Summer 1942
Commissioned	18 June 1942
Data valid for	1942
Deployment	Ladoga Lake Flotilla
Displacement	25t full load
Dimensions	10.3m oa × 3.3m × 1.1m max.
Armament	one 12.7mm MG (15t of load)
Electronics	none
Machinery	1-shaft ZIS-5 petrol engine, 75bhp
Speed	5kts
Endurance	40nm at 5kts
Complement	3 men
Fate	auxiliary since 22 Aug 1945

Following the growth of the concept of landing operations by the Russian Navy, production of 'small landing pontoons' was started in the Tallin ship repair works in 1941. However, in the face of the German advance no more than six incomplete hulls were evacuated to Leningrad. Only when frequent navigation of Lake Ladoga began in 1942 was there a marked increase in demand for small tonnage to make up supply caravans to relieve the besieged city. As a result the mass production of self-propelled tenders was ordered based on the landing pontoon design. A total of 122 tenders of 15-ton and 25-ton deadweight was built from 20 May to 12 August 1942. They were of rudimentary construction with flat hull sections and were propelled by a truck engine.

No 24 served as a transport on Lake Ladoga until the German siege was smashed, but from November 1943 on she was listed with the Baltic Fleet. Together with other tenders, deployed since January 1944 with various forces as landing craft, she was shifted to the Gulf of Finland and took part in assaults off Vyborg in July 1944. Following this she was transferred to Lake Peipus and contributed to the regaining of this area which had been achieved by November 1944.

43. The 'Series XII' *M*-class *M172* of the Northern Fleet in 1942. (Imperial War Museum, Neg No. A2244)

▲44 ▼45

44. This 'Series XIIbis' boat, *M107* (*Novosibirskiy Komsomolec*), commissioned with the Northern Fleet on 24 July 1943 and was transferred by rail to the Black Sea in 1944. By using inland waterways and railways some 1,700 minor craft were shifted between various areas during the war.

The building of four of these boats was funded by public subscription. Thanks to such enforced action, a sum in excess of 159 million roubles was collected throughout the war for the construction of sixteen submarines and 151 motor boats.

45. In 1933 the Soviet Government purchased a design of submarine from the firm Ingenieurskaantor voor Scheepsbouw in The Hague (founded by the Germans there, since submarine building was forbidden in Germany). As a result construction of the S-class 'Series IX' boats began, which influenced the efficiency of submarine design in Russia. The prototype, *SI* (*Nalim*), has been blown up in Liepaja in June 1941 to prevent her capture. (Aldo Fraccaroli)

46. In 1938 the *M*-class design was radically revised to the two-shaft, 'Series XV' of 283/350 tons, 15.5/7.9 knots, with four bow 533mm torpedo tubes and a single 45mm AA gun. Fifteen boats were laid down before the war and four were completed during hostilities. Production was continued post-war (with modifications to the bridge modelled on those of German U-boats) and 82 boats had been built by 1952. Some were transferred to satellite navies; those of the Polish Navy, seen here during the 1950s, have had their deck guns removed.

46 ▼

47. The *S*-class boats of 837/ 1,073 tons and 19.5/9 knots were armed with six 533mm torpedo tubes, and single 100mm and 45mm AA guns; *S9* of the Baltic Fleet was laid down at the inland shipyard Krasnoe Sormovo in Gorki and after her launch in 1938 she was transferred via the inland waterways to Leningrad for fitting out. She was sunk by German light forces on 5 September 1943 when trying to make her way to the open sea through the net barrier closing the Gulf of Finland.

48. Design of the *S* class was subsequently modified, first by abandoning large gunshields and later, on the 'Series IXbis' boats (seen here), by improving hull lines and conning tower. A total of 34 of this class had been completed by the end of 1945. (Official US Navy Photo)

▲47 ▼48

49. The *K*-class 'Series XIV' ocean-going submarines of 1,487 2,102tons, 22/10 knots, armed with ten 533mm torpedo tubes, two single 100mm, two 45mm AA guns and 20 mines, were the largest and undoubtedly the best Russian wartime boats. The six boats completed before the war in Leningrad were transferred to the Northern Fleet. They proved to be wet forward in the open sea so the five completed from 1942 to 1944 had a bulbous bow fitted, as seen here. (Marek Twardowski)

50. The solemn ceremony aboard *K21* of the Northern Fleet held in honour of Captain Lunin and his crew for damaging the German battleship *Tirpitz* during her action against Convoy *PQ17*. In fact, the five torpedoes fired by the Russian submarine were not even noticed by the Germans, and the hits were claimed by Lunin following two explosions reported by his hydroacoustic instrument operator. The Russian submarine service did not develop a reliable system to record hits; their captains claimed the sinking of some 87 warships and 322 merchantmen totalling 938,000GRT.

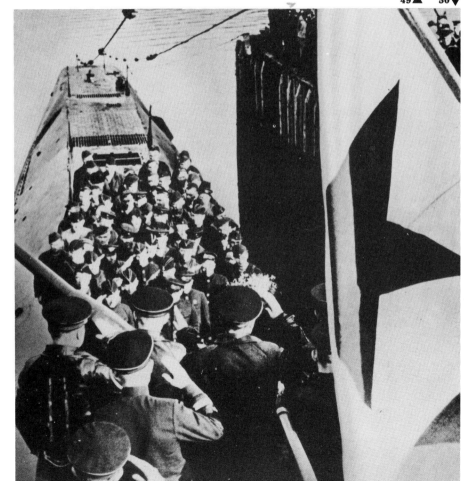

51. The Baltic Fleet *Uragan*-class guard ship with a Type 7U destroyer. (Imperial War Museum, Neg No. RUS49)

▼ 51   52 ▶

52. The *Uragan*-class guard ship *Smerch* of the Northern Fleet shown after her 1943 reconstruction, wearing a camouflage pattern specially devised to conceal her against the shore. (Boris Lemachko)

53. Fleet guard ship *Yastreb* of the Baltic Fleet in 1945. She was the prototype of the fast escorts of the 1938 Programme. Of 920 tons and 31 knots, she carried three 100mm and four 37mm AA guns, three twin 12.7mm machine-guns, triple 456mm torpedo tubes, 24 mines and 40 depth-charges. Note the sweeping gear in the stern and depth-charge racks built into the transom. Of the fifteen laid down by 1941, only two were completed during the war, and six after 1945. (Boris Lemachko)

54. The 1,760-ton, 14-knot armoured gunboat *Krasnoye Znamya* (ex-*Khrabryi*) built in 1895, was modernized from 1937 to 1939 and armed with five 130mm, three 76mm and three 45mm AA guns. She was torpedoed on 18 November 1942 off Lavansaari Island by the Finnish motor torpedo-boat *Vihuri* (formerly the Russian *N2141* of the *G5* class, sunk in 1941 but repaired by the Finns). The gunboat was raised and recommissioned in 1944, as shown here, while *Vihuri* was returned to the Russian Navy following the armistice and recommissioned as *TK80*. (Marek Twardowski)

55. The gunboat *Konstruktor* (ex-*Sibirskiy Strielok*) in 1944. She was the sole survivor of the *Okhotnik*-class 625-ton, 25-knot torpedo-boats built in 1906. An experimental vessel since 1926, she was returned to line service with the Ladoga Lake Flotilla in August 1941, with three 100mm, two 45mm AA guns and machine-guns. On 4 November 1941 her bow section was destroyed by German dive-bombers; by the spring of 1942 it had been replaced, but the boat was now 5 metres shorter because of the lack of steel. In 1945 she returned to experimental service until she was scrapped in 1957. (Boris Lemachko)

53▲ 54▼

55▼

56. Fifteen of the 59 *SH4*-class motor torpedo-boats built from 1927 to 1932 remained in line service during the Great Patriotic War. Number 64 of this class is seen here, with her crew escorting Roumanian prisoners following a sortie behind enemy lines for a 'tongue'. Commissioned with the Black Sea Fleet in 1932 as No. 66, she was renumbered 61 in 1934, then 65 in 1937, and 164 in 1940. Relegated to training duties in April 1941 as *U3*, she returned to line service in October 1941, changing her number to 184, and finally to 64 in August 1942. Note the home-made launcher for the M8-type rockets carried in the bows of the boat in the background.

▲56 ▼57

57. This *G5*-class motor torpedo-boat was commissioned into the Black Sea Fleet in 1940 as No. 185. She was renumbered 182 in August 1941 and finally became 125 a year later. She was sunk by German coastal artillery off Novorossisk on 11 October 1943. These 'Series 10' boats were powered by two GAM-34BS-type 850bhp petrol engines and could achieve 53 knots in calm water. They were armed with two 533mm torpedoes in troughs and one 12.7mm DShK-type machine-gun. During the war 73 boats of the class were lost and 31 were discarded. (Jerzy Micinski)

▼58

58. The *G5*-class No. 47 being examined by German seamen following her surrender to E-boats on 27 June 1941 off Liepaja. In July political commissars were placed in all ships of the Russian Navy to ensure the loyalty of the crews. (Jerzy Micinski)

59. The *G5*-class No. 106 of the Black Sea Fleet has a *Katyusha* rocket-launcher above the bridge.

60. The *G5*-class motor torpedo-boats Nos. 72, 82, 92 and 102 of the Black Sea Fleet, photographed in 1942. The first and third boats of this group did not survive into the following year. (Jerzy Micinski)

59▲   60▼

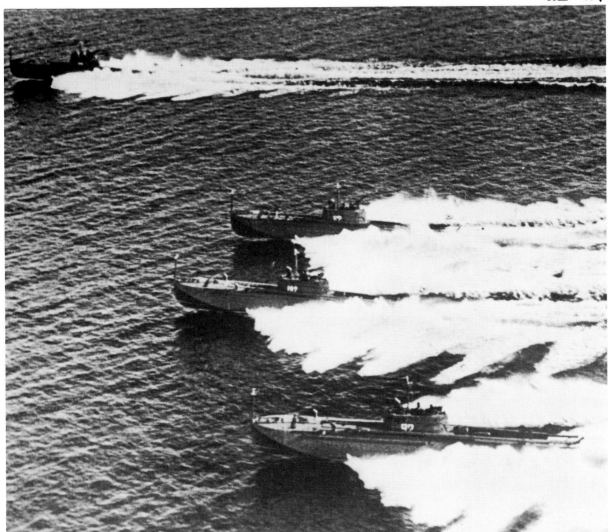

▲61   ▼62

61. Two *G5*-class motor torpedo-boats putting to sea. Note the torpedo-launching gear and the additional 12.7mm DShK-type machine-gun on the structure above. (Jerzy Micinski)

62. From the mid-1930s the Soviet Navy conducted a series of experiments with motor torpedo-boats of various sizes built either from aluminium alloy, steel or wood. This wreck of an experimental boat was photographed in 1942 off Sevastopol. (Aldo Fraccaroli)

63. The *D3*-class *TK116* of the Northern Fleet in 1944. She is carrying two 533mm torpedoes, one single and one twin 20mm gun, one 12.7mm machine-gun and eight depth-charges. She was built in Leningrad from 1939 to 1943 and was transferred to the Arctic in December 1943. She returned to the Baltic Fleet in April 1945 to be transferred to the Polish Navy the following year. (Boris Lemachko)

64. The *Komsomolec* class of 20.5-ton, 46-knot motor torpedo-boats with aluminium alloy hulls, armed with two 533mm torpedo tubes and two twin 12.7mm machine-guns, were evaluated in 1940 to replace the *G5* class, but series production was suspended until the end of 1944 because of the German invasion. By the end of 1945, a total of 31 'Series 12' boats, as seen here, powered by Lend-Lease Packard engines, had entered service. Boats of the Baltic Fleet scored some hits on the German evacuation fleet in the Gulf of Danzig during April 1945. (Boris Lemachko)

65. The *MO4*-class sub-chaser No. 125 of the Northern Fleet with landing party aboard. These small but sturdy boats were used in a variety of roles; for patrol duties, as transports or landing crafts. (Imperial War Museum, Neg No. RUS4165)

63 ▲   64 ▼

65 ▼

66. *MO4*-class boats on Lake Ladoga. Note details on boat in the foreground: aft 45mm gun, empty depth-charge racks (the enemy did not use submarines there) with smoke generators atop, and a 12.7mm DShK-type machine-gun to the right. Dazzle camouflage as seen on the boat in the background gave the visual effect of a shortened hull. (Imperial War Museum, Neg No. RUS3647)

▲66 ▼67

67. An *MO4*-class boat disabled after hitting a mine in the Gulf of Finland on 12 October 1941. (Marek Twardowski)

68. Design of the *OD200*-class wooden-hulled sub-chasers was developed in Leningrad in 1941 as a slightly heavier (47 tons) but under-engined (28 knots) modification of the *D3*-class motor torpedo-boats armed with a single 37mm AA gun, two 12.7mm machine-guns and two depth-charge racks. Production of hulls began in 1943 in small inland yards. After construction they were transported by rail to Batum for fitting out. By the end of 1944 88 boats had been completed and distributed between the Baltic, Black Sea and Pacific Fleets. Seen here is *MO328* of the Baltic Fleet in April 1946 during her passage to Poland where she was commissioned as *Dzielny*.

▼68

69. The *Artillerist* class of large (240-ton, 25-knot) sub-chasers were armed with one 76mm AA, two 37mm AA, two twin 12.7mm machine-guns and two depth-charge throwers. They entered series production in 1939, and by 1945 23 boats had been built. Production continued post-war and a further 50 boats were completed until the introduction of the *Kronshtadt* class. *BO261* of the Caspian Flotilla is seen here in 1946. (Boris Lemachko)

70. The *BMO*-class armoured patrol boat *MO622* of the Baltic Fleet entered service after the termination of hostilities. Note the simple layout of this emergency-built type. (Boris Lemachko)

71. Seventy-eight US *SC*-class sub-chasers were transferred to the Russian Navy in 1943 and 1944. *SC1486*, seen here on 25 September 1944 wearing Russian colours, was commissioned into the Northern Fleet on 30 January 1945 as *BO235*. She was scuttled in the Barents Sea in 1955 under American supervision. (US Navy Official Photo)

69 ▲   70 ▼

71 ▼

▲72 ▼73

▼74

▼75

72. *Lenin* (ex-*Shtorm*) (seen here) and her six sisters of the class of 1,100-ton, 15-knot river monitors built in 1911, were unquestioned masters of the River Amur from the late 1920s onwards, and confirmed their reputation during actions against the Kwantung Army in 1945. At that time *Lenin* was armed with four twin 120mm, two 85mm AA, two 37mm AA, six 12.7mm machine-guns and protected by a 75mm belt.

73. *Zheleznyakov* was the sole survivor of the class of six 230-ton, 9-knot river monitors built from 1935 to 1939 for the River Dnieper Flotilla. By the end of the war she carried twin 102mm, twin and single 45mm, two 37mm AA guns and three 12.7mm machine-guns. The photograph shows her preserved at Kiev where she has been on display since 1967.

74. In the face of Russian aggression the Poles scuttled all the ships of the Pinsk Flotilla from 17 to 20 September 1939. Few of them were retrieved by the Russians; an exception was a *Warszawa*-class monitor which was designated *Smolensk* class in the Russian Navy. Seen here after her salvage, she became the nucleus of the Russian Pinsk Flotilla which was formed in June 1940 but was destroyed on 28 September 1941 by the advancing Germans. (Boris Lemachko)

75. The 1124 Type 47-ton, 21-knot armoured motor gunboats of the early series production were armed with two 76mm guns in T28-type tank turrets, twin 12.7mm machine-guns and could carry 10 mines. (Imperial War Museum, Neg No. RUS693)

76. Two 1124 Type armoured motor gunboats on the Danube near Belgrade in October 1944. Note the T34-type tank turret with periscope sight on top and observation slits on the sides.

77. Number 63 and another 1125 Type armoured motor gunboat cleared for action. The cylindrical object forward of the tank turret is an armoured machine-gun turret trained athwartship. These boats were nicknamed 'river tanks'. (Imperial War Museum, Neg No. RUS3694)

76▲ 77▼

78. *BK232* and her sister, both of the 1125 Type, under way on the Danube near Vienna in March 1945. These armoured river gunboats proved exceptionally successful, and the Germans were never able to oppose them with boats of equal fighting qualities. Note the shielded twin mountings of the 12.7mm DShK-type machine-guns and the mine rails fitted. (Boris Lemachko)

▲78 ▼79

79. The *MBK*-class of sea-going armoured motor gunboat was developed in Leningrad from 1942 to 1943. These 163-ton, 13-knot boats, protected by 50mm belt and 30mm deck armour, were armed with two 76mm guns in tank turrets, two 45mm and one 37mm AA guns and two 12.7mm machine-guns. The class proved unsuccessful, being top-heavy, cramped and permanently wet forward. Only twenty were built.

▼80

80. The former imperial yacht *Shtandart*, built in 1896, was converted to a minelayer from 1938 to 1936 and was commissioned into the Baltic Fleet as *Marti*. The reconstruction was not a success as only 320 mines could be carried on her 5,665-ton displacement, while 14 knots were insufficient for an offensive minelaying capability. With an armament of four 130mm, seven 76mm and three 45mm AA guns and two 12.7mm machine-guns, she was used as a floating battery in Leningrad (seen here camouflaged as a precaution against reconnaissance aircraft). (Boris Lemachko)

87. To enable the Russians to attack Japan in 1945, the US Navy supplied the Pacific Fleet with 55 landing craft. This LCI (Landing Craft Infantry), designated *DS* class by the Russians, is seen with naval infantry aboard, but dressed for inspection rather than action.

87 ▲　　88 ▼

88. *23* or *24* (second digit of the pendant number deleted by censor), a 15-ton tender of the Baltic Fleet, is seen in 1944, loaded with men and equipment. The lack of protection contributed to heavy losses during landings against defended shores.

89 ▼

89. To overcome the lack of landing capability in the southern theatre, 150 *DB*-class 15-ton, 8.5-knot steel landing boats, capable of carrying sixty fully equipped men, were built at the inland yard at Gorki from 1942 to 1945. Forty of them were later equipped as AA defence boats. This one (preserved at Kerch) carried single 37mm and 20mm (Oerlikon) AA guns.

The *Fotofax* series

A new range of pictorial studies of military subjects for the modeller, historian and enthusiast. Each title features a carefully-selected set of photographs plus a data section of facts and figures on the topic covered. With line drawings and detailed captioning, every volume represents a succinct and valuable study of the subject. New and forthcoming titles:

Warbirds
F-111 Aardvark
P-47 Thunderbolt
B-52 Stratofortress
Stuka!
Jaguar
US Strategic Air Power:
  Europe 1942–1945
Dornier Bombers
RAF in Germany

Vintage Aircraft
German Naval Air Service
Sopwith Camel
Fleet Air Arm, 1920–1939
German Bombers of WWI

Soldiers
World War One: 1914
World War One: 1915
World War One: 1916
Union Forces of the American
  Civil War
Confederate Forces of the
  American Civil War
Luftwaffe Uniforms
British Battledress 1945–1967
  (2 vols)

Warships
Japanese Battleships, 1897–
  1945
Escort Carriers of World War
  Two
German Battleships, 1897–
  1945
Soviet Navy at War, 1941–1945
US Navy in World War Two,
  1943–1944
US Navy, 1946–1980 (2 vols)
British Submarines of World
  War One

Military Vehicles
The Chieftain Tank
Soviet Mechanized Firepower
  Today
British Armoured Cars since
  1945
NATO Armoured Fighting
  Vehicles
The Road to Berlin
NATO Support Vehicles

The *Illustrated* series

The internationally successful range of photo albums devoted to current, recent and historic topics, compiled by leading authors and representing the best means of obtaining your own photo archive.

Warbirds
US Spyplanes
USAF Today
Strategic Bombers, 1945–1985
Air War over Germany
Mirage
US Naval and Marine Aircraft
  Today
USAAF in World War Two
B-17 Flying Fortress
Tornado
Junkers Bombers of World War
  Two
Argentine Air Forces in the
  Falklands Conflict
F-4 Phantom Vol II
Army Gunships in Vietnam
Soviet Air Power Today
F-105 Thunderchief
Fifty Classic Warbirds
Canberra and B-57
German Jets of World War Two

Vintage Warbirds
The Royal Flying Corps in
  World War One
German Army Air Service in
  World War One
RAF between the Wars
The Bristol Fighter
Fokker Fighters of World War
  One
Air War over Britain, 1914–
  1918
Nieuport Aircraft of World War
  One

Tanks
Israeli Tanks and Combat
  Vehicles
Operation Barbarossa
Afrika Korps
Self-Propelled Howitzers
British Army Combat Vehicles
  1945 to the Present
The Churchill Tank
US Mechanized Firepower
  Today
Hitler's Panzers
Panzer Armee Afrika
US Marine Tanks in World War
  Two

Warships
The Royal Navy in 1980s
The US Navy Today
NATO Navies of the 1980s
British Destroyers in World
  War Two
Nuclear Powered Submarines
Soviet Navy Today
British Destroyers in World
  War One
The World's Aircraft Carriers,
  1914–1945
The Russian Convoys, 1941–
  1945
The US Navy in World War
  Two
British Submarines in World
  War Two
British Cruisers in World War
  One
U-Boats of World War Two
Malta Convoys, 1940–1943

Uniforms
US Special Forces of World
  War Two
US Special Forces 1945 to the
  Present
The British Army in Northern
  Ireland
Israeli Defence Forces, 1948 to
  the Present
British Special Forces, 1945 to
  Present
US Army Uniforms Europe,
  1944–1945
The French Foreign Legion
Modern American Soldier
Israeli Elite Units
US Airborne Forces of World
  War Two
The Boer War
The Commandos World War
  Two to the Present
Victorian Colonial Wars

A catalogue listing these series and other Arms & Armour Press titles is available on request from: Sales Department, Arms & Armour Press, Artillery House, Artillery Row, London SW1P 1RT.